WHAT YOUR HANDS HAVE DONE

T0161360

WHAT YOUR HANDS HAVE DONE

CHRIS BAILEY

NIGHTWOOD EDITIONS

2018

Nightwood Editions
P.O. Box 1779
Gibsons, BC VON 1V0
Canada
www.nightwoodeditions.com

EDITOR: Amber McMillan
COVER DESIGN & TYPESETTING: Carleton Wilson

Canada

Canada Council   Conseil des Arts   BRITISH COLUMBIA
for the Arts   du Canada   ARTS COUNCIL
                                            An agency of the Province of British Columbia

Nightwood Editions acknowledges the support of the Canada Council for
the Arts, which last year invested $153 million to bring the arts to Canadians
throughout the country. We also gratefully acknowledge financial support
from the Government of Canada and from the Province of British Columbia
through the BC Arts Council and the Book Publishing Tax Credit.

This book has been produced on 100% post-consumer recycled,
ancient-forest-free paper, processed chlorine-free
and printed with vegetable-based dyes.

Printed and bound in Canada.

CIP data available from Library and Archives Canada.

ISBN 978-0-88971-350-5

For my family:
Sometimes it's about doing what you can and fuck the rest.

CONTENTS

YOUR FATHER WILL TELL YOU

Lobster Fishing with the Old Man / 11

My Uncle the Fisherman / 12

Fisherman Tales / 13

Brandon / 14

Mary Grace / 15

Bonnie / 16

William / 17

Crow Piss: a Pantoum / 18

This Guy / 19

Tommy / 20

The Fisherman's Daughter / 21

The Actor's Wife / 22

She Was There / 23

I Hope It'll All Keep Together / 26

This Could Be It / 27

Mending Herring Nets / 28

Found Him Dead / 30

Peter / 31

Bored on the Boat / 32

You Want to Write About Love / 33

Spanish Dancing Horses / 34

Have a Cookie / 35

A SLOW PROCESS

A Slow Process / 39

THE MORSE CODE OF BLINKING TAIL LIGHTS

Pillow Talk / 65

Bachelor Party Blues / 66

Early Morning / 67

A Bliss / 68

Kiss and Go: a Tanka / 69

When it Rains / 70

August 1988 / 72

How Could You Forget This? / 73

The Dream / 74

The Things You Tell Yourself / 75

Toronto City Streets / 76

Beetles Running Mad / 77

In the Mountains / 78

Autumn Evening / 79

The Place That's Held You / 80

Uncle Stormcloud / 81

Soon the Frost'll Settle / 82

Snow Is Falling / 83

She Wants to Make Sure You're Sure / 84

Her Ringless Finger / 85

Your Father's Rope / 86

Like Warren Zevon / 87

The Drop / 88

They Step in Time / 89

Acknowledgements / 92

About the Author / 95

YOUR FATHER
WILL TELL YOU

LOBSTER FISHING WITH THE OLD MAN

He didn't care what state you were in,
who you took home Friday night,
or if condoms ever shielded your dick
from accidental family trees. Like the one
you fell from, cradleless and too small
to live, hungry for something no one
ever managed to give you.

No, your father cared only that you
show up on time, ready to brave the cold
spring Atlantic; toss lobster in their pans,
sober enough to measure properly;
remember to check for spawn.

MY UNCLE THE FISHERMAN

Michael has nicknames for everyone
and everything. Sea urchins are whores'
eggs. Elmer Charlie Ivan is The Crow
'cause you can't leave nothing shiny
with him. Brandon is Shithead Shortcock
and someone else is named Ten Rows
of Teeth. Michael's beard is the colour
of dreary clouds and his eyes are forever
hidden by sunglasses. He smokes constantly.
He sneezed once, and quoting an episode
of *The Simpsons* I told him sneezing
was just his soul escaping and by saying
God bless you, I'd crammed it back in.
He told me to go fuck myself.

FISHERMAN TALES

I'm worth more dead than alive,
your father says two drinks in.
Glass of moonshine, touch of tap water.

He moves onto Dan Ramsay. How Dan
sobered up a day, just one day,
then did himself in. His wife

having to get one of the MacKenzies
to push open the workshop door and there
he was, backline around his neck.

You can't believe it.
The man had his problems, yes,
but Jesus. Your father finishes his drink.

Stares at the grease-smudged glass. Says,
There's more of that happening
than you know about.

BRANDON

At his third going-away party, drank beer,
smoked smokes with the owner of the only
Chinese restaurant in Souris. Brandon heading
west on his own terms, to BC, not to Alberta
to bitch seismic cable as your brothers before,
or to work electrical like Mary Grace's ex.

There was a storm a few nights before when
he pointed his rig to the west'ard. Thunder like
hoofbeats, gunshots. Lightning cracked the shell
over the island, sky veined like ice against the poles
in spring, used to get to the lobster gear when
the winds don't blow right after winter. *Imagine*

what it would be like back in the day, he said.
A storm like this. You'd think the world was ending.
The two of you beneath the eaves of your childhood
home. Rain coming down like beer shits from
the weekend of a hard week. Not knowing what to say,
you agree, refuse the cigarette offered to you.

MARY GRACE

burns bridges with brothers as though
she can read ashes like tea leaves to know
more than everybody else. One of two
redheads, her fists were hardened in high school
halls. Fighting is what your family is good at.
She socked Brandon in the jaw for buttering
her nose when she turned seventeen.
She cried after her first day at the fish plant
in Souris, and now sits in a house in Stratford
with two kids and a husband yet to come home.
Waits for results from some crystal guru
in Charlottetown to find out what food she can eat.
Like the rest of your family, Mary Grace
is not all bad. When you first learned to read
she had you say the words from a magazine ad,
I just got my first period. Ask her.
She's probably still laughing about that.

BONNIE

shook shit out of raw lobster tails at the plant
then cared for her kid brothers, changed the diapers
Brandon and you filled. The oldest child left
alive after Peter passed, and when your parents
sold their catch, came home with bodies perfumed
by sunlight and seawater, old bait dumped over the side
and blown back at them, your mother'd tear a strip
out of her for not cleaning the house. Saturday
mornings, Bon would ask to check her numbers,
the lotto results in a blue box onscreen. She played
everyone's ages, the faith in her family never returned.
The channel reverting to your cartoons after.

WILLIAM

Your brother's never done a wrong, never
admitted half as much. Sinless as a post-baptism
newborn. This man who fired you, called you
useless because he didn't take care of the building's
loft when he should have. Wanted to wrench it free
with still-wet traps drying below, hundreds more
in the drive waiting to come in. Will won't apologize.

Gives you a card, three hundred in cash a year later
at your makeshift going-away party. Says if you
need anything, ask. *Just ask, okay?*

His eyes look to the watercolour sky, now blue,
now purple and red. His penance in your hand,
weighted one lonely dollar at a time.

CROW PISS: A PANTOUM

Sit and listen, and your father will tell you
how it is. Up before
crow piss. Before daylight breaks
between the branches. *Get up and see*

how it is. Up before
your brothers who sleep shit-faced.
Between the branches, get up and see
the ocean, the world that birthed your grandfather,

your brothers who sleep shit-faced
till noon. Day half done and they're in the hay.
The ocean, the world that birthed your grandfather,
it wells in the lungs. Keeps you still

till noon. Day half done and they're in the hay.
Crow piss. Before daylight breaks.
It wells in the lungs, keeps you still.
Sit and listen. Your father will tell you.

THIS GUY

This guy I've seen pick fights with evening shadows.
Drank till two a.m. then drove to some chick's place

to screw before heading out at four for a twelve-hour
day slinging lobster traps on the Gulf of Saint Lawrence.

This guy who lost a father but still joked. Lost a father
and saw the dark for what it was, then came back.

Strapped on shoes he wasn't sure he'd grow into,
but fuck it. A fella needs something for his feet.

This guy who found sobriety for a bit, maybe even Jesus,
found a woman who makes him crazy. He sits in front

of me holding his newborn son, white hospital shades
rattling behind. His son makes these soft dream noises

in his sleep. This guy's grinning now, saying nothing
and it's like those shoes were meant for him.

TOMMY

A hard man to get along with, Tommy'll
read this and know it's true but *Fuck, Christopher,*
you're a goddamned city-slicker now, whatdoyaknow?
You never fought like he did. "Tommy Gun," named
for his hands hard like fibreglass, like lead weights
on the end of mackerel lines. He palmed a lobster trap
like a basketball when loading the boat for Setting Day.
Coffee in the other hand, lit cigarette loose on his lips.
Set the trap down at the wharf's edge and burned
that smoke back as though it was filled with regrets—
the debt he don't speak of, the plane that takes him
from his kids he don't get the chance to know.

THE FISHERMAN'S DAUGHTER

Moves with a sureness not seen in girls
raised from the earth and taught what's
beneath your feet will always be there
for you. Her legs, long and slender, lithe
stepping over the drunks strewn about
this place, this house party, this seaside
town with its broken streets and dead end
promises of something more than a chance
to draw pogey while the less fortunate stand
nude with Gibran, facing the wind, melting
into the sun, and she steps over the threshold,
her legs carrying her to me. Her smile like
coming home after an oil patch winter, like
putting the last trap on the stack of a long
Landing Day or finding a twenty thought
forgotten in a pocket. Outside the horizon
burns with settling dusk, the air thick with
cigarette smoke, torn mad by the buzzing
of mosquitoes. In the house she reaches out
to me but I'm not ready to come home
and winter clouds linger in the distance.

THE ACTOR'S WIFE

Violently beautiful, a barrage of cliché:
bombshell, breathtaking, drop-dead.
I need a real man in my life, she says,
her words soft on the summer heat,
rising through years of dismay and nights
of boredom as her lips brush against
my ear. The unwashed texture of her hair,
her skin smells of three hours departed
from the beach, burned by the sun.
With sore shoulders, a back stiffened
by the weight of herring nets, I tell her
she's in luck. *I even shave sometimes.*

SHE WAS THERE

I

Thinking about her still makes you hard
sometimes, though you're not interested
anymore. As if your dick rises from obligation
more than love or lust, or boredom.

She was there, cooked for you. Helped clean
the mess you'd become from decades
spent on your father's ocean hauling lobsters
from its depths, gulping down the sea air.

Even when the booze was too much,
she knew you were more than the vomit
caked to your shirt. Less than confessions
made beneath the red summer moon.

II

And *she* was there too, all fire
and crazed with belief in you—
the kind that lets movie heroes triumph
over greedy dragons, 'roid-riddled Russians,
the self-doubt that can cripple
worse than a car wreck.

Her conversations about scaling heights
too terrifying for you, about crying
while reading Auden kept you
going when your back hurt. When
it spasmed against a six-hundred-pound
mackerel tank, her voice soothing wounds

from barbed hooks. She didn't ask for a thing
though you wanted to give her all
you were, knowing it would never be
enough, someone else already claiming her
while you washed blood from your eyes,
scrubbed scales off your tired arms.

III

It shouldn't be possible to love more
than one at a time, but you do.
Not with your cock, but with your heart
that manages to beat, even on sober nights

when, beneath unsteady starlight, you ache
for a sleep so long it'd be as if you ceased
to exist and the world wouldn't know
the failures you've wrought.

If you shut your eyes, you can see them.
The women who kept you together
when your world wrecked on a jagged
skerry no birds have songs for.

I HOPE IT'LL ALL KEEP TOGETHER

Your father's hoped this all his life. The childhood
he don't speak of save the barn chores, the house's draft.
The time his nose got broke by his brother Michael
when they used frozen cow shit as a hockey puck.
Years later, married with children. The fishermen
said if he didn't stop lobster fishing they'd sink his boat,

burn his fucking house down. He told them, *Go ahead*,
but they'd have to sail back in and he'd be waiting,
shotgun loaded to blow their heads off.
He hopes it'll all keep together. It managed to
when he lost his first child, thirteen-year-old Peter
with diabetes and liver failure and all that. Even after

the drinking your father did, the drinking he did
for years, it all kept. Now in his sixties he hopes
it'll still keep. His right knee is new, the left needs
replacing. He's had both shoulders done, his back,
and don't mention the charley horses anymore,
or the lump on his neck the doc said's probably cancer.

His joints are swollen, rusted with arthritis.
His eyes are going now, too. Bits of his field
of vision's fading or just not there anymore.
All he says to you is, *I hope it'll all keep together
for a little while yet*, and sips his tea, eyes pointed out
the west kitchen window watching the sun go out.

THIS COULD BE IT

My father saying, *Get out here, Chris. This could be it.*
Get out here and have a look before we all go to Hell
and I come from my room and glimpse him through smoke
that's not curling, just swarming, my father saying,
This could be it. Check it out before it blows, nodding
toward the furnace, its rattling and clanging and banging,
angry vibrations through the cold cement floor, the gauges
saying the pressure is soaring, the temperature's near
two hundred, Dad saying, *You might want to grab*
your stuff and get out before it's too late and I remember
Bukowski said, *There's nothing worse than too late*
and I'm close enough to my father to smell the moon-
shine and Mountain Dew, see the glassy finish over cataract
clouds and notice his shirt is gone and the relentless furnace
refuses to go unheard, its beating swan song of fire
and steel and fear and smoke while I grab my things—
an old notebook, a half-written letter, a creased picture
of my niece, my wallet and jacket and car keys—no time
for boots or underwear or that book signed by Gaiman,
and against a carelessly frigid spring sun, outside I stand,
the shadow of him, inside, waiting for the end.

MENDING HERRING NETS

In an old purple loveseat your father sits
sewing herring net twine shredded on an anchor
the night before. You don't know enough
to be proper help, so you sit, listen. Sometimes
this is all he wants, someone to laugh at his jokes.

I ever tell you about Darcie Fisher? he says.
Horse seller. No good for much else. His hands
move steady, the knife blade glints in the dust-
choked workshop light when a knot is made.
This guy goes to him looking for a horse.

Darcie says, Shit, I got just the one for you,
and goes into the barn, brings out this big beast,
this huge animal, and it's knocking hell out of
everything on its way out the doors. Sweat beads
on your father's forehead. Outside the dirt-

streaked window over his shoulder, the sky
is afire with the late summer sunset. A country
crooner sings through the static of the radio.
The man tells Darcie, look, I ain't buying that
goddamn horse off you. He's blind as a bat.

Your father relaxes in the chair. Springs strain
as he leans back. Rests his hands on his knees.
He always wears long pants, denim; you've never
seen the skin of his legs. They probably glow
in the dark. *Darcie turns to the horse,*

then back to the man and says, blind?
This horse ain't blind. He just don't give a fuck.

FOUND HIM DEAD

They found Marcus dead in his chair
ten years after his sister was found in the run
of Basin Head. Ten years after he hooked
a hose to his exhaust at North Lake Harbour,
his car so rusted, so chewed up by saltwater,
he couldn't stop his breath. *They found him
dead in his chair*, your father says. *Don't know
if he had a heart attack or did himself in.*

PETER

Known only to Brandon and to you as a face
whose smile helps paper the walls, never fading.
Peter is your grandfather's name, the name
of your father's friend killed in a game of chicken
before you or Brandon or Peter were even accidents
waiting to happen. The life your family led
before you. The one glimpsed a bit every April
and every October. The weight you cannot
know to bear, the name all you can manage.

BORED ON THE BOAT

You form stories in your head. A house
haunted by tulpas. An assassin meeting another
in a small town's only motel. A man,
a detective, practises his cross draw in the mirror,
realizes his age. Tells himself
maybe some men are best shot in the back.

Your uncle Michael sees this, says, *Come on
now, Philly-fucky. Get to it!* The trap
on the washboard is full at both ends. Michael
built it over winter in his workshop with the moon-
shine still in the corner. *I built this trap*, you say.
Look at the lobster. This is one of mine.

Jumped up jingling Jesus Christ, he says. *You
wouldn't know how to set a fucking mouse trap.*

YOU WANT TO WRITE ABOUT LOVE

You want to write about her but can't.
Not the way you want. When you think
of her, what you know is her smell. Her taste.
Your knees burning against hotel bedsheets
as you enter her again. The soreness
of your cock after the third night of this.

The stain left from the night before.
Her saying maybe you should leave so she can
walk tomorrow. Saying that, if you want,
you can fuck her in her ass and cum on her back,
her tits, in her mouth. She wants to know
your flavour, wants to lick you off her skin.

You want to write about loving her unlike
all the others. About that first kiss you shared,
basking in streetlights filtered through descending
snow, the vague suggestion of mountains
in the dark. The way she touched your arm,
your hand, brushed your cheek in passing.

SPANISH DANCING HORSES

She brushes her hair beside me.
No mirror, just brushing, says
she wants to get this knot out.
Yesterday she spoke of Spanish
dancing horses, the word *beautiful*
tumbling from her lips and she
leaned in as she went on
about these horses, how they moved,
the stamina they must have.
I didn't follow but I listened.
There's a pole, I think, or a lance,
and that's how the rider guides
the horse, like a hand on the small
of a woman's back when the lights
are low and the band is on and Sinatra
sings. Pulling me from my daydream,
she calls me by the wrong name.
Smiles, apologizes. Says his name again
and I wonder if she's ever said my name
like that. Accidental, a slip of the tongue,
if she's ever said it like she described
the Spanish horses, their dance.

HAVE A COOKIE

The way your father tells you is simple. To the point.
Speaking with the tone he'd use to say the direction
of the tides, what your brother Tom in Fort Mac said,
or describing the noise the truck axle makes.

His hand on the thing sprouting from his neck:
*The doctor says it's probably cancer. They're cutting
it off next week.* A strip of paper towel in front of him.
A cup filled with tea. A new pack of cookies that rattles

when he reaches in, not looking at you. He endures
your stunned silence, says, *I asked if he had his pocket
knife on him, said he could do it right there
if he wanted.* Then: *Sit down, boy. Have a cookie.*

Not knowing what else to do or say, you sit.
Take a cookie. The kind with icing in the middle. One
half vanilla, the other chocolate. He fills ice cream
dishes with these for long days on the boat.

Something to snack on when working in the sun.
You snap the cookie in two, then four, and stare
a while at what your hands have done.

A SLOW
PROCESS

A SLOW PROCESS

I

Grammie's in the hospital.
She had a heart attack
and she's not doing good.
That's what the doctors say.

> *Jesus Christ.*

Listen, boy, she's ninety-three.
She did goddamn good to make it
this far along, the way people
been dropping around here.

II

Smoke blooms and swirls from stacks
standing like white-grey trees against the ink
of sky and fog of Charlottetown's city lights.

We're allowed to go only one-oh-five, max—
Will's rules issued from out west.
It's his car we're in, after all. Tommy,
Mary Grace, Bonnie and me.

When he sees us, Dad'll be so surprised.
We're all civil for now, even Tom and Mary Grace
(though they aren't talking much).

We'll get there when we get there.
If Grammie decides she don't want to wait,
I won't hold it against her.

III

Dad shouldn't be alone but it's all
he can want, watching Grammie in bed now,
her body a thin shelf for a blue blanket,
her breathing laboured like God's

as He carved the Earth, painted the skies,
watered the seas, wondered at the magic
of clay and air, and light-bearing stars
that fall beyond the window in this room

where the walls are uniform and a curtain
dangles, useless like a suicide decorating
an ash tree and I'm curious:
did Dad lose his glasses on purpose

so he wouldn't clearly see her go like this,
a hallway and twelve years separating
her from her husband?

IV

Dad wants to go to the TV room, so we sit,
chuckle at NBC's footage of Russia hosting
the opening Olympic ceremony.

Then Dad says it's a slow process, dying.
A waiting game now. That's all this is.

A painting on a dull wall depicts a woman
who may be pregnant. Her arms enfold a child,
hers, I think. The sun caresses their hair, their faces,
kisses their forms to life while red clover
blossoms in the shrubs around them.

V

There is talk of wills now. Tommy's mad
Dad hasn't brought it up since Dad was dead drunk
on Christmas Eve. Madder still if someone

were to get more than him, monetarily or sentimentally—
the fleet with its berth, the house in need of new
siding and the dead apple tree in the yard.

The painting hung in our grandparents' kitchen.
Tom's quiet, his hands busy with the Bic
and loose change in his pockets.

VI

The sun tries to hide but still shines
through shredded feathers of clouds.

The radio says tomorrow will be the same:
fair but cold. I just want Dad to know that.

VII

Sitting at the computer desk at home
listening to "Mohammed's Radio" play,
answering phones while Dad and Mom
meet the priest to make the arrangements.

A woman from Ontario called. I met her
once, a lifetime ago, when pop came in
plastic cups and cookies were store-bought,

and when cousin Jimmy played guitar,
singing of the provinces and their capitals,
Elmira was always the capital of Prince
Edward Island. It's been Charlottetown

since Grampie died. She asked for Dad,
didn't know about Grammie, not till I told
her. She's sorry. She'll call back later.

VIII

Mary Grace is fretting over the phone:
Did you hear? Did you cry like I did?
Her voice trembles like the ocean waters
Dad has harvested for lobster, mackerel,

tuna, herring, his sanity. An ocean
she didn't brave often, despite what she says
during her theatrics, or what benefits
she reaped from the sweat of his back,

the snapping of his shoulder tendons.
Why is my sister so heartbroken?
Did she not stage her wedding hours away
so Grammie couldn't attend? To avoid

photos with the shell in the wheelchair?
She once asked me to come along to visit
Grammie so she wouldn't be alone with her.
Can't you hear her asking that?

IX

Brandon left his girlfriend in Nova Scotia
early to make it up home on time but death sweeps
through like wind in these snowy February fields,
and though they may have danced in the sunrise
this morning, the trees are all still now.

She wasn't supposed to see Saturday, I tell him,
but she did. Lasted till Sunday. Maybe even
saw sunlight once more. Almost too stubborn
to go, but she went anyway.

Brandon's admission: it's not Grammie he came
to see, but our father. He says this softly and dips
his grilled cheese in a mess of ketchup, thinks
possibly of the fresh pack of smokes in his car.

X

Dad wakes up early. Has tea.

Most of a biscuit laden with refrigerated peanut butter.
Heads to the cemetery.

Times are tough and the church can't afford to clear
snow from the graves.

Come summer, grass grows wild with no money to cut it.
The tractor starts without protest.

The journey is slow, forming a path for her, orange
wooden hockey sticks as markers.

XI

We're up home with Mom around the kitchen
table. Brandon is eating. Mary Grace and Bonnie
talk about waking Peter twenty-six years ago.
I recall an overcast day. Gulf waters lapping
at the washboards as Will and I haul lobster gear.
Will telling me Dad's broken promise, the drinking
done after saying he wouldn't anymore.
Mary Grace remembers her lips brushing against
her oldest brother's forehead as she kissed him
goodbye, four at the time. Tommy's never said
a thing to me about it. Not even once.

XII

Dad's brother Michael, the one
he still talks to, paces the funeral home
making awkward jokes, farting
and saying, *Now did you hear that one?*

We're in the costumes we have
for these things—suits or black on black.
Ties intermittent.

Dad's other brother, my godfather,
won't speak to me. Does he speak
to my father? Does he still hold a grudge
from the time I was five and flipped
him off, not knowing what it meant?
Doesn't he know I'm sorry?

XIII

My calmness surprises the priest who laughs
at something I say about my childhood,
about Brandon going through a phase of not liking
old people. We're standing beside her and it
really is like she's sleeping, but frightened. Maybe
not frightened, but troubled. Why else would she
hold those red rosary beads so tight to her chest?
I don't tell the priest, but it's refreshing, the idea
of burying someone on the far side of fifty.
The last one was twenty-one. The priest takes
my hand firmly: *God bless you, my friend.* I thank
him and he's off to shake more hands. Someone says,
She looks so good. Dad agrees. I look at her once
more. It's the lips. They never get the lips right.

XIV

There's a black-and-white photo
of my grandparents getting married.
I've never seen it before now,
central in a collage Mary Grace
put together. My godmother says,
That's seventy years ago.

They're younger than I ever
imagined. Grammie is my age, early
twenties, and beautiful. Grampie
looks strong. No hint of the cane
he'd need later, no rumour of the grey
that would take his black hair
like thick smoke.

That expression on their faces,
standing on those church steps,
I haven't seen it like that, unbridled
as they show it. Delight. Happiness.
They may even be sober.

XV

Over the stereo system, a lone piano plays
amid the movements of gentle ocean waves
and the sound the wind makes as it massages the limbs

of trees, kisses the hardened faces of mountains.
Dad's next to my godfather because my godfather
refuses to sit next to Michael.

They don't speak to each other. No words.
If looks are exchanged, they're slight, secret. A knife
taken to trap twine or backline in the dark.

In their chairs, angled to be the furthest apart possible,
a lobster trawl with the rope stretched, singing
tight between the traps.

The door creaks. There's the stamping
of feet and we all stand.

XVI

We gather for the final vigil. Some of the women
are crying, red rings even the eyes of the older boys.
We're asked to join hands and I hear Dad chuckle
at my godfather's offering, but he accepts the two

crooked fingers. With what lies ahead, what does it
matter what lies behind, that mess with the house
after Grampie passed? What does twelve winters ago
matter when a new one blankets your doorstep?

XVII

Day two at Dingwell's and Tommy still hasn't entered
the room with Grammie. Mary Grace makes Bonnie
go with her and they stand over Grammie whispering
before pressing their lips to her forehead. This is goodbye.

Dad was the first here. No one would see him bid her
farewell. I imagine he had Mom wait in the car while he did.

Michael lingers, walks back and forth, touches Grammie
with his fingers, his palms, as if trying to heal her.
He cradles the end of the blue cloth inscribed with the logo
of the CWL. My godfather stands with his wife and son,

their prayers silent. Michael paces past, cracking for
a cigarette. I overhear Dad say this is how it's meant to be,

a child burying a parent and Mary Grace asks if I've gone up.
I wasn't planning on it, I tell her. She tells me I should
say goodbye, take my younger brother with me. It's our last
chance, she says. I relay to Brandon what she said. Since we

were kids, we've done the tough things together, but he refuses
to go up. I don't press the issue, and so I stand alone.

Looking down I want to take her hand, hold her once more.
It's been years since we touched. I didn't visit last Christmas,
didn't take her hand as she lay in bed, one foot in the river
of Temperance, the other on the far bank. It's too late now.

Is this guilt? It must be. There's no room for anything else.

XVIII

One of six grandsons, I carry her
to the hearse. She's so light, if I relaxed
my grip just a little she'd float away.

This almost seems a trick. The blue
casket looked so heavy as people shook
our hands and gave us their blessings,
their prayers. Our grandmother feels
less than a basket of fresh lilies.

XIX

A few cars unknowingly merge
into our formation as we drive from Souris

to St. Columba. The sky is a solid wall
of grey, a shade lighter than my father's

eyes. Snow hedges the roadsides and the wind
pushes through, making the going slow.

We take the long way, through Elmira.
Brandon casts a sideward gaze to the small house
where Dad was raised. Does it again,
swerves a little before correcting himself.

XX

The undertaker materializes
as the service wraps.
His phone rings, hasn't stopped
since we got to the church.
Dad never says a thing.

XXI

I near trip over a headstone, but we finally
get her next to Grampie. We're asked to stand
with our families so I stand with Brandon
while the priest does his thing.

I glance over. Dad's off a little on his own,
his suit stark against the winter graveyard. Sparse
snow spirals about us. His eyes are no longer
weary, yet he's the most worn I've ever seen.

The wind is raw. Minus twenty-one
and Dad don't seem to notice.

XXII

Dad pours a round of 83 and I refuse
at first and then take a glass. Liberal whiskey,
little water, no ice. One drink done in one motion,
the first in over a month, but I stop at that.

He's drunk when I leave, and clouded
with a kind of happiness I know is transient. That
shadow is there. As I reach the door I hear him
say gently, *That's it. An end to suffering.*

XXIII

I head to Bonnie's and we talk about death
a while. She says Grammie looked good,
repeats this a couple times and I don't argue.

She has Will on speaker. They both ask
after Dad. I tell them he's good. Better
than expected but drinking.

Will says some nice things about family,
I just don't know if he believes them.
Mary Grace and him aren't speaking.

Maybe he's feeling lonely stuck out west.
Our conversation is interrupted
by Bonnie's daughter. Three years old,

Kayla wants milk. Then she wants a hug.
I don't want to let her go.

THE MORSE CODE OF BLINKING TAIL LIGHTS

PILLOW TALK

She says she's scared the city
will change you, swallow you up,
steal you away from her.
Says this in bed at the Super 8.

Sunlight falls through a part
in white curtains. On TV,
the country has fallen into
a *technical recession*. She says

this is how she likes watching
the news. *You're perfect like this.*
Her ear pressed to your chest,
listening to the tremor of your blood.

BACHELOR PARTY BLUES

I'm the best man at the bachelor party trying to get a hooker
to dance for the groom-to-be, telling him, *I'm going to find
someone to floss their ass with your face* while calling every
whore-peddler in the book: *Hello, I'd like to procure an escort*

for a small bachelor party of four gentlemen, getting responses
like, *None tonight* or, *We've got one, but she's busy right now.*
The man of the hour says, *You shouldn't have said "procure."*
They probably don't know what it means; you spooked them.

The hockey player staring at the cop-to-be says he's gonna
be up front with her—*She walks in, I'm gonna say, Hey,*
I am going to fuck you. Christ, Thursday night in a city
of thousands and nary a harlot to be had in this overpriced

hotel room with lamps bereft of shades or working bulbs.
Hard beds, windows that don't open. Pouring another drink
the defenceman says, *Try Pandora's Box again, see if that*
girl is free now. I pick up the phone. I dial.

EARLY MORNING

The sun skirts the city skyline. On a train to you.
Tired maples, buildings that could be homes flicker past
as the bruised sky heals blue.

Do you remember when I'd describe the skies
above my island to you? The shredded feathers of clouds
in the north, the cool touch of dusk to the east. On the water,
the chalk horizon that separated us.

Out this window, tree limbs twist like broken ribs
in mid-November. A cloudless sky. You soon to be
an arm's length away or closer.

A BLISS

You want to tell everyone about her hand
tracing your thigh but you can't. Not in this moving
car, barrelling past man-made trees and ponds.
Sculpted shrubbery. Highways inscribed
on the earth: glyphs, sigils, invocations of a world
you can't fathom or grasp or believe. The Morse
code of blinking tail lights. You say three words
to her. She says them too and this city is made
of cement and steel and glass. It shines so brightly
you can't see, don't want to see anything but her.
So you focus instead on her hand, her fingers
laced in yours. The absence of her wedding ring.

KISS AND GO: A TANKA

We spend too much time
saying goodbye at trains. Kiss
and go. The sun slung low
on the horizon as we part. Air
cooling. Kiss. Go.

WHEN IT RAINS

I

On nights he can't sleep, he thumbs
through letters from her. Works them flat
on the chipped kitchen table. She wrote
about little things, past things. Being wrought
with anxiety when called on in school,
and he sees her standing before the class,
bashful and too quiet. It's the small things
she shares that make him want to touch her
once more, hold her through the night,
darkness slipping around them.

He writes about big things. Future things.
The house he will build, the money he'll make
if the magazines, the publishers will open
their eyes and give him a chance. The people
will love him, can't they see? (She can see.)
Rending lobster in the cannery only pays
so much, affords him his stamps and envelopes.
Pen, paper, milk and eggs. The occasional bottle
of beer. This room where he goes over her words
like a boy tracing an earned wound that will
someday be a scar he displays with pride,
saying, *Look what I have left of her.*

II

On his days off he hitches to town, walks
the main drag, takes note of each face he sees.
Reflects on those living beyond what he knows,
what the townsfolk know. He wonders if those
with lives bigger than his would be jealous
of his view of the lighthouse standing dim
on a prim point of land and crowded by a mob
of evergreens. Sometimes on these walks,
it rains. Water falling so hard it is almost a mist
against the surfaces with which it collides.
He takes shelter, the whole time seeing her
silhouette made of rain on that first stroll
through her mother's garden. Feels her tug
on his hand, hears her laughter through
the drum of rain upon the roofs and treetops
as she pulls him into the small barn. Her
body appearing to him then as it does now,
a ghost made of flesh scented by scattered
raindrops. Her lips on his, the pulse of her
beating against the palm of his hand. He drank
her sweat, sipped autumn showers from
the nook of her collarbone. When it rains
while he's in town, he seeks shelter where
he can. Lights a cigarette, waits for it to pass.

AUGUST 1988

Your grandmother speaks of August '88,
your grandfather in bed. His last laughs
coming down the wood-panelled hall
of their home. The stroke that dropped
his left side, rendered it useless, left him
a lobster trap with the heads cut and no
time, no ability to sew things back.
Uncle Bobbie called her to the room.
Your grandfather's slow breaths. Before
this: half carrying him to the bathroom,
lantern light, wiping his ass, the bathing.
Him saying, *Dammit, Margie, just let
Him take me.* She remembers how
his breathing stopped before the leaves
turned red, the sky gunmetal grey, mere
months before your own brother passed.
He was gone, this man who spread cold
molasses on hot biscuits. Your grand-
mother prayed, what else could she do,
she says. *What can you do? Times like
that. Times like that, you pray.* When
his body was taken away, she washed
the bedclothes, wiped the walls clean
with hot water and vinegar. Her short
dark hair, sleeves rolled to the elbows,
hands on her hips, upset at him for
leaving her to wash everything herself.

HOW COULD YOU FORGET THIS?

Don't forget where you came from. Simple.

Easy like dropping a slut rock tied to a herring
net off the boat's stern, sidestepping rusted

chains skidding past your feet against the deck's
worn floor. So many boats on the water
at night, your father calls it a city. Curses

the Bruces for using anchors instead of stones.
They shred the nets, fuckers, using those things.
The pain in your back, your arms, from a night
spent shaking nets. Herring piled past your ankles.

Brandon forgot to open the hatches. Thirty
minutes sleep in forty-eight hours. Set and haul
back while herring blocks blood red on the sounder.
Your father telling you, *The work is hard
and the smell follows you but the money don't*

stink, now, does it? That bathing after work
knocks a few scales off. How could you forget
this? Now with your first-ever Starbucks coffee,
facing a four-storey wall of greenery as it filters
the air in this school building. Clean air in your
diesel lungs, a book in your softening hands.

THE DREAM

Us at the kitchen table. Coffee in mugs, steam rising,
sun streaming through the window at your back. You
reading the paper and me peeling an orange. My nails
weren't long or sharp enough, so I slid a knife tip along
the orange's centre, skin splitting neat beneath the blade.

I removed the peel and juice squirted out. It got my cheek,
my shirt. I looked over to see you grinning at me,
then laughing. Then I'm laughing. That was the dream.
Breakfast, sunlight, the juice of an orange. The two
of us laughing like that. You putting your hand on mine.

THE THINGS YOU TELL YOURSELF

You get told growing up you can do anything,
whatever the fuck you put your mind to. Christ,
you got the brains, don't you? Whisper this
in the dark, easy and sure as the Lord's Prayer.

Make a list of everything you'll do and say. All
that'll be accomplished. Do it like that. You've got
Elvis's birthday so you're a rock star tearing through
the ragged fabric of a sonic space. Read everything

Gaiman's written so that Nebula and, dammit,
Hugo belong to you. And it's okay to drink like
your father after he lost a son, then a mother. If your
hands get dirty or the knuckles split against the chin

of someone knows less than you, blood thickening
black on your skin, fine. That's what soap's for. Wash
away another night, let it trace the contours of the drain
and aim for a better day tomorrow. All this and more.

TORONTO CITY STREETS

People move slow on the sidewalks of this place.
You say hello to a woman walking and she treats
you like the homeless man crouched by the LCBO

on Queen West. A face in the crowd, a pothole
in the pavement. One more tire on the fire
of humanity, its tread wore to nothing. Above you,

a few flakes of snow tumble past windows
where no one looks out. At your feet, a man asks
for the change you never seem to have.

BEETLES RUNNING MAD

The beetles hit the floors in this basement
the ceilings hit the walls like frustrated fists
clicking as they go *click click click click*
they scurry into the dark of this room
with its walls they hit (the walls are blue; man
are they blue) in this stagnant summer heat
Stravinsky plays over their hurried steps,
plays over those riots in Paris, Igor is playing
to the schoolboy Zevon while Bukowski
is discovering his god in a Los Angeles library,
discovering the gentle madness of the line,
the way of the word written with *feeling*
while here the pipes leak water, unloved
by oil furnace warmth and released by coffee-
coloured tiles *drip drip drip drip* and there
are no girls here tonight only beetles running
mad and dying and I've killed three so far,
a fourth's wings *buzz* beneath the weight
of its body, its heavy black body, and my
jealousy is for an end that'll come soon,
the waiting here stretches beyond treelines
as the time spent here can encompass
the head of a match and now Stravinsky's
heart has failed, Zevon's lungs have quit,
Bukowski's bluebird has poison blood
and they bury what's left of Fante in the LA
dust and maybe some part of me is failing more
than my attempts to escape this feeling of being
almost home, deep down part of me could be
failing, frayed like an old shoelace fallen apart.

IN THE MOUNTAINS

Snow falls through amber streetlights
and she wants to stand out, ankle-deep
and cold, shiver against the mountain
breath laced with ice and a winter on its
way as she smokes the joint you watched
her roll from bed. She is seven different
kinds of naked; you are the same. In
your head, there's the unusual shape,
the imprint the two of you leave in forming
drifts. Sweat hardening to frost in your
hair: cool, crackling along your skin.

AUTUMN EVENING

We dress after, all smiles and eyes.
I lean against the doorframe, buttoning
my shirt. You're cross-legged on the rug,
lipstick in hand. I catch your grin
in the dressing mirror. This is it.

This place, where the temperature
has cooled but the air's not as crisp
as the falls spent in Souris. Traffic
on the streets, always. Strange shadows
clogging up a sky that used to be big.

There were stars up there once.
But here there is you and there is me.
A bed, creaky floorboards, your breath
in my ears. There is you and there
is me, and all the rest out there.

THE PLACE THAT'S HELD YOU

You don't need to look to the stars
to feel small. Insignificance is found
downtown, at the foot of the CN Tower.
There's nothing up there, anyway—all
haze and rigid constellations squared
against the silhouettes of buildings.
To the east, a place that was home
falls into disrepair in a nest of rust-
coloured potato fields and smashed
glass bottles. The place that's held you
so long. The pockmarked bedroom door.
The bodies of your dog and cat beneath
the lobster traps you stacked out back.

UNCLE STORMCLOUD

He caught your brother Peter
gambling with your cousin in her room.
Tossing a new quarter for old two-dollar
bills. The man may've even raised
a hand. That's unclear.

This man who don't speak
to your father, your family, you.
Not intentionally. You've seen him
at the wharf, walking with his bum hip,
his bad back. That laugh that sounds
like your father's.

His evening ritual: tea, a biscuit
with a bit of peanut butter. The silence
of his kitchen. That west-facing window.
Eyes pointed to the sun caught in tree limbs,
the grooves of his old boat building
as the light goes out.

SOON THE FROST'LL SETTLE

On the phone your father sounds
out of breath. In the woods before
sun-up and back after it sunk down.
Talks only in terms of work:

No mackerel, not even off the bank
where the south side opens up
and the weather's piss poor. The Roses
are starting at the potatoes this week
but, no, he won't be digging.

Gotta get things put away up here
in case they call to do my shoulder.

He asks if you're liking it, the city,
with its skyscrapers and shrunken sky.
You say you haven't even had time
to stop and smell the flowers. *That's*
the expression, right?

You damn well should, he says. *Soon*
the frost'll settle and there'll be no
more flowers to be smelled.

You agree, say your goodbyes, hang up
and walk east where home rested, where
it does sometimes still. The scent
of newly cut cedar on your shirt, gum
of fresh sap on your forearms.

SNOW IS FALLING

She's leaving you early to beat the storm
and doesn't say goodbye, instead hands over
two words, gently, like a newborn at the hospital
[*her name*] though you've already forgotten
and the hangover will kick in soon and there's
no Advil or bourbon and your cock is sore
and your friend is in the ground—what, three
months now—and you still hear his voice
reviewing the new Van Halen album, *You see,*
its main problem is Van Halen isn't a very
good band, and snow is falling beyond navy
curtains and dusty blinds and frosted panes
falling from an ashen sky, the same sky she
strolls under and maybe she's humming a *good*
song as she stops to pet a golden lab, abandoned
for humping the wrong leg, sniffing at the wrong
crotch (who hasn't) and snow is falling
around moving cars, starving birds in flight
filling in silhouettes of small absent angels.

SHE WANTS TO MAKE SURE YOU'RE SURE

Another kiss-and-you-don't-want-to-go.
She talks about girls she's interviewed
to babysit her daughter, uses the words
young and *beautiful* and you want
so bad to kiss her again, to describe
the feeling of looking over your shoulder
to see her making soup for lunch.
That smile she gave you as sunlight slanted
in at her back. You want so bad to pull
that feeling, full and whole, from your pocket
and put it on the dash so she can see
but you can't so you stare out the window
at cars stalled in traffic, their colours
diminished by the grey November light.

HER RINGLESS FINGER

She doesn't wear the ring with you
but she sometimes speaks of him. Fond
recollections of their shared memories,
the home that will not hold you. May
in PEI and there's frost in the hollows,
still lingering. Cribbage by kerosene
lantern light while the sky clouds over
in the south of Ontario. The time your
father said, *You're doing good*. Try
and let those things comfort you.
The sensation of her. Forget him,
photograph-close and smiling; wonder
if the poet can hide the cracks in his
walls behind the piss-poor paint job
of alliteration. Forget the photo. Remember
her ringless finger. Her hand in yours.

YOUR FATHER'S ROPE

You want to write something different
but can't. Take the rope, fathom it out
and you'll see how little slack there is.

A fourteen-hour drive is nothing
to the salt-crusted coils that hold you.
Tradition. The way your uncle Michael
puckered his lips so his cigarette became
a smokestack, him a slow-moving train.

The tapping of rain on your oil jacket.
The diesel rotting your lungs and your hands,
how they seize up in the cold. Twenty-four
and all the aches and pains of your sixty-
two-year-old father. You are his son.

This is his rope, his anchor. Either holding
you back or keeping you safe from changing
tides. But you know about anchors.
They shred nets, and those around you
catch just as much, or less, as you.

LIKE WARREN ZEVON

Remember the nights you tried to live
like Zevon, all whiskey and women
and avoidance. Living in the LA streets
of your mind, a four-letter world
with palm trees instead of pine. When
you were just an excitable boy, not
naming the women whose sisters
loved you, accidentally, like martyrs
in the arrant darkness by abandoned
railroad tracks. Remember the women
leaving, wakes of perfume trailing
as they smiled, you tied to them
now in ways that don't make sense.
Remember drinking like a desperado
but unable to slake it completely,
the thirst that's killed so many of your
brothers, hating yourself for it. The liquor
flooding the space between you and those
around you. The distance grown vast
and freezing, a tundric waste where sunlight
on snow is too much for even the birds.

THE DROP

Scared of heights and seven floors up
and you think, shit, this drop could kill you.
Not high enough to blend you like pastel

into the street exactly, but enough to keep
your heart from thumping tomorrow.
Sit out here, watch the lights on the broken-

toothed horizon. Question why you're here
without a sea to collapse into, or rust-red soil
to dust your bones, stain your tired flesh.

THEY STEP IN TIME

The blacktop is burning in April. An old
woman gingerly crosses the street to the grocery
store. She is slower than Christ walking the Via
Dolorosa and it's burning, this island, melting down
to the sandstone and the dog shit holding it together.

They step in time like this: a stiff but sure shuffle.
Words whispered between leaning bodies
like dust vanishing between shafts of sunlight.

WHAT YOUR HANDS HAVE DONE

ACKNOWLEDGEMENTS

Thanks to my parents, Arnold and Nancy, for feeding and watering me all these years and doing all that they do for me and my siblings. There aren't enough thanks to give them what they deserve, and they are not thanked often enough.

And to my siblings whose names I used for characters in this book, thank you. Some of your actions, as I'm sure you know, are how I observed them, while others, along with your interior motives, are entirely made up.

A big thanks to my writing professors and mentors that have helped me improve and grow as a poet and writer. Without the careful guidance and consideration of Deirdre Kessler, Richard Lemm, Lorna Crozier, Dionne Brand and Liz Philips, I wouldn't have made it this far along. What you've all done and continue to do means so much and I've been so lucky to work with you.

Thank you to Catherine Bush and my University of Guelph MFA cohort, particularly Julie Mannell who told me I should submit to Nightwood as the deadline was yesterday.

Thank you to the two Banff Centre poetry cohorts that gave me feedback on a chunk of these poems.

Thanks to my writing group on PEI. I think I started this in the right place?

Thanks to Silas, Amber, Nathaniel, Carleton and the Nightwood crew for believing enough in this book to make it a real thing you can hold in your hands.

And thank you to George Elliott Clarke, Catherine MacLellan, Joseph Millar, Jen Villamere and anyone else who I've forgotten and has put up with these poems and this book along the way.

Some of these poems have appeared in different forms in *UPEI Arts Review*, *Villamere: the lowbrow magazine of high-end CanLit*, gritLIT's *How Exhilarating and How Close* and on CBC Radio's *Mainstreet PEI*.

ABOUT THE AUTHOR

Chris Bailey is a fisherman and award-winning author from North Lake, Prince Edward Island. He has a MFA in Creative Writing from the University of Guelph and is a past recipient of the Milton Acorn Award for poetry. His work has appeared in *Villamere: the lowbrow magazine of high-end CanLit*, *The Puritan's Town Crier* and the UPEI *Arts Review*, and on CBC Radio. He splits his time between Hamilton and North Lake.

PHOTO CREDIT: BRADY MCCLOSKEY PHOTOGRAPHY